Monsters

Written by Sarah Prince

Illustrated by Marjory Gardner

sundance™

I have big eyes
to see everything.

I have big ears
to hear everything.

I have big teeth
to eat everything.

I have a big nose
to smell everything.

9

I have big arms
to grab everything.

I am a monster.
I am coming to get you!